PIGS

Jason Little

Grolier
an imprint of
◧ SCHOLASTIC
www.scholastic.com/librarypublishing

Published 2009 by Grolier
An Imprint of Scholastic Library Publishing
Old Sherman Turnpike
Danbury, Connecticut 06816

For The Brown Reference Group plc
Project Editor: Jolyon Goddard
Picture Researchers: Clare Newman, Sophie
Mortimer
Designer: Sarah Williams
Managing Editor: Tim Harris

Volume ISBN-13: 978-0-7172-8052-0
Volume ISBN-10: 0-7172-8052-7

**Library of Congress
Cataloging-in-Publication Data**

Nature's children. Set 5.
     p. cm.
  Includes index.
  ISBN-13: 978-0-7172-8084-1
  ISBN-10: 0-7172-8084-5 (set)
  1. Animals--Encyclopedias, Juvenile. I.
Grolier Educational (Firm)
QL49.N386 2009
590.3--dc22

                        2008014674

Printed and bound in China

Contents

FACT FILE: Pigs

Class	Mammals (Mammalia)
Order	Even-toed hoofed animals (Artiodactyla)
Family	Pigs and boars (Suidae)
Genus	*Sus*
Species	Domesticated pig and wild boar (*S. scrofa*)
World distribution	Domesticated pigs live on farms throughout the world; wild boars are found naturally in Europe, Africa, and Asia
Habitat	Domestic pigs are kept in sheds or pens, and some graze on pastures; wild pigs live in forests or on plains
Distinctive physical characteristics	Plump body, short legs, coarse hair, short tail, small eyes, and a flat nose
Habits	Pigs sniff out food, which they dig out of the ground; they roll in mud to protect their skin
Diet	Domestic pigs eat cereals, such as corn, wheat, barley, and oats, and animal food; wild pigs eat leaves, roots, fruit, and flowers, tree bark, insects, worms, and other small animals

Introduction

Pink fleshy skin, a naturally plump body, large ears, a flat-ended snout, **hooves**, and a curly tail make the pig one of the most easily recognized members of the animal kingdom. But pigs actually come in many different colors, markings, and sizes. They also have different personalities depending on their kind, or **breed**.

Pigs often appear as fun-loving characters in books and movies. But the term *pig* is often used to mean greedy, gluttonous, and unclean. In fact, pigs are intelligent and delightful creatures.

Some types of pigs are very hairy.

All members of the pig family, including these warthogs from Africa, have four toes on each foot.

History Lesson

Pigs belong to a group of hoofed mammals that have an even number of toes on each foot. Some of the other animals in this group include cattle, antelope, camels, and giraffes. Scientists believe that pigs originated in Asia about 30 million years ago. From Asia, they spread to Europe and Africa.

The scientific name for the pig family is Suidae (SOO-EE-DAY), and it contains 16 species. The members of the family include wild **boars** and domesticated pigs, warthogs (WORT-HOGZ), bushpigs, the babirusa (BAH-BUH-ROO-SUH), the pygmy hog, and the Indochinese warty pig.

Humans first domesticated wild boars about 9,000 years ago in the Middle East. These early farm pigs—and the knowledge of how to domesticate them—spread across the world as different peoples **migrated**. In Europe, farmers began domesticating the local wild boars. Eventually, these European pigs replaced the farm pigs originating from the Middle East—possibly because their meat tasted better.

Wild Cousins

Wild pigs are often called boars. This word is also used for a domesticated male pig. Wild boars still live in the forests of Europe and Asia, as well as on the plains of South Africa. They have also been introduced to many other parts of the world, including North America.

The wild boar looks quite different from its domesticated relative. It has short, bristly hair that is usually black, brown, or gray. Adult wild boars range in length from 4½ to 6½ feet (1.3 to 2 m) and weigh up to 770 pounds (350 kg).

Wild boars live in groups called **sounders**. Sounders usually contain about 20 animals. For most of the year, a sounder contains **sows**, or female pigs, and their young, or piglets. Adult male boars usually only join a sounder when they want to **mate** with the sows.

Wild boars are nocturnal, or active at night. During this time, they search for food. Wild boars eat a wide range of foods, including acorns, fruit, chestnuts, potatoes, roots, dead animals, worms, insects, lizards, and birds.

Wild boars were hunted by people in prehistoric times. In fact, cave paintings as old as 35,000 years have been found showing wild boars and hunters.

To a female pig,
a truffle smells like
a male pig during
the breeding season!

10

Working Pigs

Humans have raised pigs for many different purposes. Pigs have been raised for meat, to do work, and as pets.

In ancient Egypt, pigs were used to help plant seeds. When the pigs walked across the planting area, their hooves made holes just the right size for the seeds that were planted.

Pigs were used during ancient wars to scare the enemies' war elephants. The elephants were frightened of the pigs' squeals and would turn around.

To this day, sows are used to sniff out truffles in forests. Truffles are types of wild **fungi** that grow underground in parts of Europe and Asia. They are a highly prized **delicacy**, or special food. A pig's sharp sense of smell allows it to locate the truffles and dig them out. Before the pig gets a chance to eat the truffles, the owner takes them away.

Think Pink!

Pigs are often thought of as being overweight, dirty, greedy, lazy, and stupid. In fact, pigs are none of these things.

Being plump is natural for a pig. During winter, pigs put on an extra layer of fat to help them keep warm. Of course, pigs like to **wallow**, or roll around, in puddles of mud. But they do that because it helps them keep cool. Unlike humans, who sweat all over to cool down, pigs only sweat through their snout. Pigs aren't greedy—they are large animals that need a lot of food. Perhaps the idea came about from the way pigs eat—sniffing out food and eating it noisily. Pigs are not at all lazy. They might rest much of the day, but they are often active at night, like their wild ancestors.

Pigs are one of the most intelligent mammals—more intelligent than an average dog. Pigs can dream, recognize their name if kept as pets, and herd sheep. They communicate with one another, using about 20 different types of sounds.

Pigs have a great memory. That is very helpful in the wild. They have to remember where and when to find good sources of foods.

Free-range pigs are usually fed natural foods that are free from chemical additives.

Farm Life

In ancient times, domesticated pigs were kept inside buildings to keep them from escaping and to protect them from their natural enemies. Some ancient farms kept more than 1,000 pigs!

A few hundred years ago, farm animals, including pigs, lived in the same houses as people. If the home had two stories, the animals often lived on the first floor with the people living above.

In recent years, modern technology has changed the way pigs are farmed. Pigs are often kept in large metal sheds called **intensive piggeries**. The sheds are cleaned and the pigs fed and watered automatically by machines. These pigs are fed on food designed to make them grow quickly and stay healthy. However, many people believe that this lack of a natural life is not good for the pigs' well-being. Today, there are **free-range** farms. There, the pigs can choose when they want to rest in a shelter or roam freely in a large field.

To Market

Most pigs are raised to become meat for humans. In fact, the meat from pigs, or **pork**, is the most popular meat in the world—more so than poultry, such as chicken and turkey, and beef from cows. Pork is especially popular in China and Europe. In the United States, roast pork and ham are the most common types of meat from pigs.

Many nonfood parts of the pig are used, too. The pig's bristly hairs can be used to make paintbrushes. The skin is often turned into leather to make boots, shoes, gloves, saddles, watch straps, and footballs.

About 60 million pigs live on farms in the United States.

Traditionally, pigpens were next to the farmhouse. That meant the farmer did not have to walk far to feed the pigs. They were usually given the leftovers from his family's meals.

Pigpens

The small enclosure that many domesticated pigs are kept in is called a sty, or pigpen. Pigpens are usually found on small or family-run farms. A typical pigpen has an outdoor space and an indoor area. The outdoor space is enclosed by a fence to keep the pigs from escaping. The indoor area provides shelter and somewhere for the pigs to sleep.

The outdoor area is usually bare dirt. Pigs like to dig or root for food in the soil. The ground is usually bare because the pig will eat any plants that manage to start to grow!

Pigs especially like muddy areas in the pen. These allow them to cover themselves in mud. On a hot day, rolling in mud not only cools a pig down, but also protects it from the sun and biting insects. That's because a coating of mud acts both as a sunscreen and a barrier against pesky insects.

Different Breeds

Pigs can be either pure breeds or **crossbreeds**. Purebred pigs have parents that are both of the same breed. Crossbreeds have parents that are two different breeds.

Different breeds have different sizes, skin color, and hair length. There are many kinds of pigs on farms or in piggeries in the United States. Popular breeds in the United States include the American Yorkshire pig and the Hampshire. The American Yorkshire pig is fair-skinned. It was bred from British Yorkshire pigs that were brought to the United States in the early 1800s. They are hearty and easy to care for. The Hampshire pig also first arrived in the United States from England in the early 1800s. These pigs are black with a white band of skin around the middle of their body.

However, most pigs on farms are crossbreeds. These pigs tend to grow faster, stay healthier, and weigh more than purebred pigs when fully mature.

American Yorkshire pigs are common throughout the United States. This breed produces a high proportion of meat.

Although smaller than most American farm breeds, pot-bellied pigs, such as this one, can weigh up to 300 pounds (136 kg).

Big Pigs

A pig's size is one of the most important things for a pig farmer. When the farmer sells his or her pigs, the larger their size the more money the farmer will usually make. Crossbred pigs are often the largest and fastest-growing types of pigs. More recently the trend has been to breed pigs that are "lean," which means they yield more meat and less fat.

Some pigs reach an enormous size. One of the largest pigs on record weighed slightly more than 1 ton (1 tonne)! Most adult pigs weigh less than one-quarter of that weight. This gigantic pig was called Big Bill and was a Poland China pig. Poland China pigs are very popular in the United States because they are big, feed well, are easygoing, and produce large **litters** of piglets.

Pigs as Pets

Because pigs are intelligent, clean, and can be housebroken, they can be kept as pets. But, of the many different breeds of pigs, only some are suitable as pets.

In Vietnam during the 1960s, a breed of small pig was developed from various other breeds. This new breed was called the Vietnamese pot-bellied pig. It is smaller than other breeds and grows to about 3 feet (0.9 m) long and 15 inches (38 cm) high. Adults usually weigh about 125 pounds (56 kg).

Young Vietnamese pot-bellied pigs are very small and friendly, which is why they are popular as pets. However, they grow to be fairly large and bulky.

An even smaller pig has been bred from the New Zealand kune kune (KOO-NEE KOO-NEE) pig. As adults, these pigs weigh about 46 pounds (20 kg). That's about one-fifth of the weight of an average adult pig. They are also easy to housebreak and have a friendly nature. They make excellent pets.

House Pigs

Pigs can be housebroken easily and will eat almost anything. But there are important things to consider before getting a pet pig. It will require daily exercise, a lot of attention, and also patience. A Vietnamese pot-bellied pig can live to 15 years, so having one as a pet is a long-term commitment.

Many people who buy a pet pig as a piglet abandon the animal when it reaches full size. That's because the owners do not realize how large and heavy the pig will become!

Because pigs are smart, a house must be made pig-proof if a pet pig spends any amount of time indoors. Pigs can learn to open cupboards and refrigerators using their snout, so any doors they can reach must be made secure. Electrical outlets and cords need to be securely covered. A pig will investigate anything on the floor and probably try to eat it! Pigs might chew on shoes, houseplants, and newspapers.

Pigs are also commonly
called hogs or swine.

Living Together

Would you like a pig as a pet? If you answered yes, you need to think about where it will eat, sleep, exercise, and relieve itself. You will also need to provide a pool of water or muddy area for the pig to wallow in when the weather is hot.

Pigs are **omnivores** [OM-NEE-VORZ], which means that they eat both plants and animals. In the wild, they get their protein from insects, worms, and dead animals. Special pig feeds are available for pet pigs that contain all their dietary needs.

Like other pets, a pig needs its own space and a place to sleep. An area should be chosen before the pig moves in and decides for itself! A warm area with blankets will usually do. A pig's bed should be away from the area where it relieves itself—they are clean animals. Allowing the pig to roam around a yard or taking it for walks will help keep it fit.

This pet pig is a Goettinger mini pig. It has formed a close attachment to its owner, who trains pigs for work in movies.

A pet pig needs daily exercise. Specially made pig harnesses help when taking a pig for a walk!

Training Pigs

Pigs can be housebroken, just like dogs. It is best to housebreak pet pigs when they are young. They have a very good memory, so they will never forget once trained. While training a pig, the owner should be gentle and kind, but firm. The pet should be rewarded with healthy food treats when it does something right.

Pigs can climb stairs easily when they are young, but it gets harder for them to climb as they get heavier. Steps place stress on their joints, which can eventually lead to injury. If a pig needs to go up a few steps to get in and out of the house, it should be given a ramp to use, instead. Placing treats at the top of the ramp or along it will help the pig get used to using the ramp.

Pig Brother

Pigs are herd animals. When a pig is kept as a pet, it sees the humans it lives with as part of its herd. A pet pig might try to become the "boss" in its "herd" by trying to dominate young children!

If there are other family pets, it is important to be sure a pet pig will get along with them. Pigs are normally fine with cats, but dogs have been known to attack pet pigs. Therefore, pigs and dogs should never be left alone together.

Pigs, however, can be kept with pet birds. Unlike cats, pigs cannot climb or jump high. Pigs are quite strong and can easily knock over furniture, so a birdcage should be placed somewhere high and made very secure.

Pets that grow up together usually get along without fighting.

Pigs need to drink a lot of water. They will always need a trough or bucket of freshwater.

34

Food for Pigs

Wild pigs eat a wide range of foods, including leaves, grasses, roots, fruit, flowers, insects, worms, dead animals, and tree bark.

Farm pigs are usually fed twice a day. They are given grains, such as barley, corn, oats, and wheat, as well as greens and dried food made from meat. The food is designed to ensure that the pigs put on weight and grow quickly. Farm pigs are often also given vitamins and minerals, as well as medicine, to keep them healthy and to protect them from diseases.

Pet pigs should also be fed twice each day. They should not be given "human" treats, such as chocolate—in fact, chocolate is harmful to many animals, including pigs.

Rooting Around

Pigs love to root around—using their snout to dig for tasty roots and buried bark. Rooting is a natural behavior for a pig. A pet-pig owner should not try to stop a pig from rooting.

A pet pig will also eat leaves, vegetables, and flowers if it has a backyard to roam around. In fact, it is a good idea to fence off part of the yard just for the pig. Otherwise, it will eat or destroy almost all of the plants! If a pig spends a lot of time indoors, a "root box" is useful to keep the pig busy. A root box could contain dirt or rocks covering hidden food.

A pet pig can be just as demanding as a pet dog. It might follow its owner around the house and yard. Pigs love affection. They love to have their ears rubbed. Another way to please a pet pig is to provide a pool during the summer for the pig to wallow in. Wallowing is another natural pleasure for a pig!

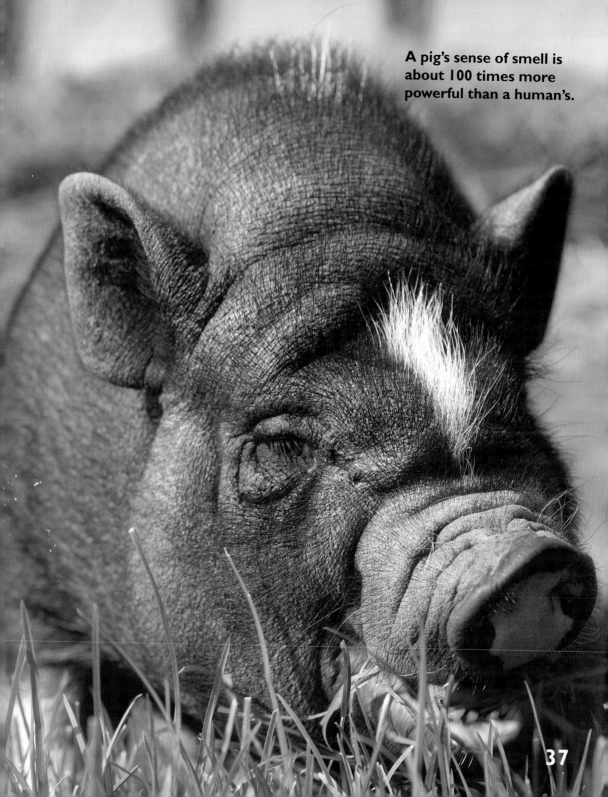

A pig's sense of smell is about 100 times more powerful than a human's.

A vet checks to see whether or not a sow is pregnant.

Keeping Healthy

Pig farmers need to keep their animals as healthy as possible. The best ways to keep pigs healthy are to provide them with a good shelter, clean water, the right kind of food, and room to exercise.

Any disease of farm pigs is usually dealt with quickly before it spreads to other pigs or farms. Loss of appetite is usually the first sign that a pig is sick. An ill pig is usually given medicine and watched closely to make sure that its disease does not spread. Nowadays, many farm animals are **vaccinated** to prevent disease in much the same way that vaccines are given to children.

Herd Life

In the wild, pigs live in herds of up to 50 pigs. In most animal herds, there is a **pecking order**, and that is the same in a group of pigs. There will be a top pig, a bottom pig, and many pigs in between. The higher up a pig is, the better access it will have to food and the better its chances to mate.

The pecking order becomes disrupted when a new pig joins the herd—both in the wild and on farms. There are usually fights to determine the new order. Fights between pigs sometimes last for a few hours. They charge at each other and bite. All pigs have large tusklike teeth toward the front of their mouth. Pigs with large tusks can cause serious injuries. However, the fights rarely end in death. Eventually, one opponent backs down, and the winner keeps or betters its rank in the pecking order.

Pigs communicate with one another by snorting and squealing. Soft snorting shows that they are happy. A pet pig usually makes these sounds when being petted or when rooting or eating. A pig squeals when it is hurt or frightened.

Two young pigs fight to improve their pecking order among a group of farm pigs.

The babirusa eats
leaves and fallen fruits.
Unlike other pigs, it
does not root for food.

Bizarre Babirusa

Among the most unusual members of the pig family is the rare babirusa, which lives in Sulawesi and surrounding islands in Indonesia. It is one of the oldest living types of wild pigs. It split from its relatives more than 20 million years ago.

Male babirusas weigh up to 220 pounds (100 kg). The sows are smaller. The boars have two pairs of tusks, which curve backward over their head. These tusks are their **canine teeth**. They grow to 12 inches (30 cm) long. The upper canines grow upward, piercing through the animal's snout! The lower daggerlike canines are used for fighting other males. The upper tusks protect the animal's face during fights.

Some babirusas are almost hairless and others are covered in bristly hairs. They have gray-brown coloration, which keeps them hidden in their damp forest and **canebrake** home.

Babirusas have some habits very different from other pigs. Female babirusas give birth to just one or two young at a time. Babirusas are active during the day. Some even swim in the sea!

Pigs and Medicine

A pig's internal **organs** are similar to those of a human's. Therefore, they are often used in medical research. A pig's heart is particularly useful for research because it is similar in size and structure to a human heart. Heart valves are structures that control the flow of blood into and through the heart. Pigs' heart valves have been used to replace faulty heart valves in humans. The valves last about 15 years before needing replacement. In addition, surgeons have also transplanted a pig's liver into a person with liver disease as a temporary organ until a suitable human liver became available.

Some people do not want animals to be used for medical research. Other people think it is important to use animals to find cures for diseases. What do you think?

These piglets are clones—identical copies of one another.

A litter of piglets sometimes includes a baby smaller than the others. This piglet is called a runt and has less chance of surviving than its littermates.

46

A Litter of Piglets

After mating with a boar, a sow is pregnant for about four months. She usually gives birth to a litter of between 6 and 20 piglets, depending on the breed of pig. Piglets are born fairly well developed. Their eyes are open—unlike cats and dogs—and they are soon walking. The piglets **nurse** on their mother's rich milk. A piglet usually weighs about 3 pounds (1.4 kg) when it is born. Piglets grow fast. After only three weeks, a piglet might weigh nearly four times as much as its birth weight.

Farm piglets are weaned—have their milk diet replaced with solid food—at about four weeks. However, in the wild, piglets nurse for much longer—up to 15 weeks.

A piglet should stay with its mother for six to eight weeks. For the first two weeks, piglets cannot make their own body heat. During this time, the mother keeps her litter close to her body to keep them snug and warm.

4-H Pigs

Many students in the United States undertake 4-H projects. Among the most common projects is the 4-H market hog project, in which students raise one or more pigs for market. The students provide their pigs with a home and shelter, supply straw or other bedding, and give the pigs food and water each day. They also check their pigs' health regularly and make sure they are vaccinated. It takes about four months for piglets to grow to a weight—about 230 pounds (105 kg)—suitable for market.

The 4-H market hog project teaches the students how to look after a farm animal responsibly. The students also get to learn firsthand about these fascinating and gentle animals. In addition, some students may get to show their pig at an animal fair. That involves learning to walk a pig in front of the judges. With luck and good care, the pig may even win a prize!

Words to Know

Boars	Wild pigs or domesticated male pigs.
Breed	A type of pig.
Canebrake	An area where sugarcane grows thickly.
Canine teeth	Pointed teeth toward the front of the mouth, two in each jaw. In some pigs they grow into large tusks.
Crossbreeds	Animals that are a mixture of two different breeds.
Delicacy	A rare or special item of food.
Free-range	Allowed to roam around a field; not confined to an indoor pen.
Fungi	Life-forms that include yeasts, mushrooms, and molds.
Hooves	Large, tough nails that cover the feet of pigs, horses, and many other mammals.
Intensive piggeries	Farms in which many pigs are kept in large metal sheds and are fed and cleaned automatically.

Litters	Groups of baby animals born to the same mother at the same time.
Mate	To come together to produce young; either of a breeding pair.
Migrated	Traveled a long distance to live somewhere else.
Nurse	To drink the mother's milk.
Omnivores	Animals that eat both plants and animals.
Organs	Internal body parts, such as the heart, lungs, and liver.
Pecking order	The rank, or status, of each animal within a group.
Pork	The meat from pigs.
Sounders	A group of wild boars.
Sows	Adult female pigs.
Vaccinated	To protect an animal or human against disease.
Wallow	To roll around in water or mud.

Find Out More

Books

Hudak, H. C. *Pigs*. Farm Animals. New York: Weigl Publishers Inc., 2006.

Miller, S. S. *Pigs*. True Books. Danbury, Connecticut: Children's Press, 2000.

Web sites

Mammals: Warthog
www.sandiegozoo.org/animalbytes/t-warthog.html
Information about the warthog—a wild relative of domestic pigs.

Pigs, Swine, or Hogs
www.enchantedlearning.com/subjects/mammals/farm/Pigprintout.shtml
Facts about pigs and a diagram to print.

Index